SCIENCE
MAGIC
WITH WATER

CHRIS OXLADE

BARRON'S

First edition for the United States, Canada, and the Philippines published 1994 by Barron's Educational Series, Inc.

Design
David West Children's Book Design
Designer
Steve Woosnam-Savage
Editor
Suzanne Melia
Illustrator
Ian Thompson
Photographer
Roger Vlitos
Model maker
Keith Newell

© Aladdin Books Ltd. 1993
Created and designed by
N.W. Books
28 Percy Street
London W1P 9FF

First published in
Great Britain in 1993 by
Franklin Watts Ltd.
96 Leonard Street
London EC2A 4RH

All inquiries should be addressed to:
Barron's Educational Series, Inc.
250 Wireless Boulevard
Hauppauge, NY 11788

International Standard Book No.
0-8120-6448-8 (hardcover)
0-8120-1986-5 (paperback)

Library of Congress Catalog
Card No. 94-5548

Library of Congress Cataloging-in-Publication Data

Oxlade, Chris.
Science magic with water / Chris Oxlade. — 1st ed. for the U.S., Canada, and the Philippines
p. cm. — (Science magic)
Includes index.
ISBN 0-8120-6448-8. — ISBN 0-8120-1986-5 (pbk.).
1. Conjuring—Juvenile literature.
2. Water—Juvenile literature. 3. Scientific recreations—Juvenile literature. [1. Magic tricks. 2. Water. 3. Scientific recreations.]
I. Title. II. Series.
GV 1548.099 1994   94-5548
793.8—dc20   CIP
                                        AC

Printed in Belgium
4567 4208 987654321

CONTENTS

WATER MAGIC!

Water is the most common substance on Earth. You probably use water every day without realizing what strange and magical properties it holds. Water can store energy, travel uphill, and fill the gaps in other materials. It can even support some objects on a thin, flexible skin that covers its surface. Water can travel around corners and cause other substances to magically disappear on contact. It is the natural star of your magic show.

BE AN EXPERT MAGICIAN

PREPARING YOUR ROUTINE

There is much more to being a magician than just doing tricks. It is important that you and your assistant practice your whole routine lots of times, so that your performance goes smoothly when you do it for an audience. You will be a more entertaining magician if you do.

PROPS

Props are all the bits and pieces of equipment that a magician uses during an act, including his or her clothes as well as the things needed for the tricks themselves. It's a good idea to make a magician's trunk from a large box to keep all your props in. During your routine, you could dip into the trunk, pulling out all sorts of equipment and crazy objects (see Misdirection). You could tell jokes about these objects.

PROPS LIST

Magic wand ★ Top hat ★ Vest Binder clip ★ Candle ★ Candy wrappers with stars ★ Cardboard, thick and thin ★ Cardboard boxes ★ Cellophane tape ★ Cotton balls ★ Craft knife ★ Dishwashing detergent ★ Drill ★ Eggs ★ Food coloring ★ Funnel Glass bowl ★ Glass vase ★ Glasses (tumblers) ★ Glue Large plastic soda bottles, one with cap ★ Paints ★ Paper, white and colored ★ Ping-Pong ball ★ Plastic container ★ Plastic glasses ★ Plastic tubes ★ Salt ★ Scissors ★ Sticky putty ★ Straws ★ Thread ★ Turntable Water ★ White tissue paper ★ Wire coat hanger

WHICH TRICKS?

Work out which tricks you want to include in your routine. Put in some long tricks and some short tricks to keep your audience interested. If you can, include a trick that you can keep going back to during the routine. Magicians call this a "running gag."

MAGICIAN'S PATTER

Patter is what you say during your routine. Good patter makes a routine much more interesting and allows it to run more smoothly. It is a good way to entertain your audience during the

slower parts of your routine. Try to make up a story for each trick. Remember to introduce yourself and your assistant at the start and to thank the audience at the end. Practice your patter when you practice your tricks.

MISDIRECTION

Misdirection is an important part of a magician's routine. By waving a colorful scarf in the air or telling a joke, you can distract the audience's attention from something you'd rather they didn't see!

KEEP IT SECRET

The best magicians never give away their secrets. If anyone asks how your tricks work, just reply, "By magic!" Then you can impress people with your tricks again and again.

WHAT YOU NEED
Thick cardboard
Scissors ★ Wire coat
hanger ★ Craft knife
Ping-Pong ball
Water ★ Cellophane tape
Thread

INTRODUCING MAGIC MANDY
AND THE
MEMORY BALL

Magic Mandy waves her wand to give the Memory Ball the power to remember!

Ask for a volunteer from the audience. Demonstrate how to spin the Memory Ball (using a finger and thumb). Ask your volunteer to spin the ball, let it spin for a few seconds, and then stop it (and keep holding it). Now touch the ball lightly with your wand and say, "Remember, Memory Ball." When your volunteer lets go, the ball begins to spin again — the same way every time.

THE SCIENCE
BEHIND THE TRICK

When the ball is spun around, the inside surface pulls the water around too, so the water gradually begins to spin. When the ball is stopped, the water inside keeps spinning for a few seconds. If you let go of the ball before the spinning stops, the water makes the ball spin again. The water keeps spinning because it has inertia. This property makes things difficult to start or to stop. Heavy things, such as cars, have a great deal of inertia.

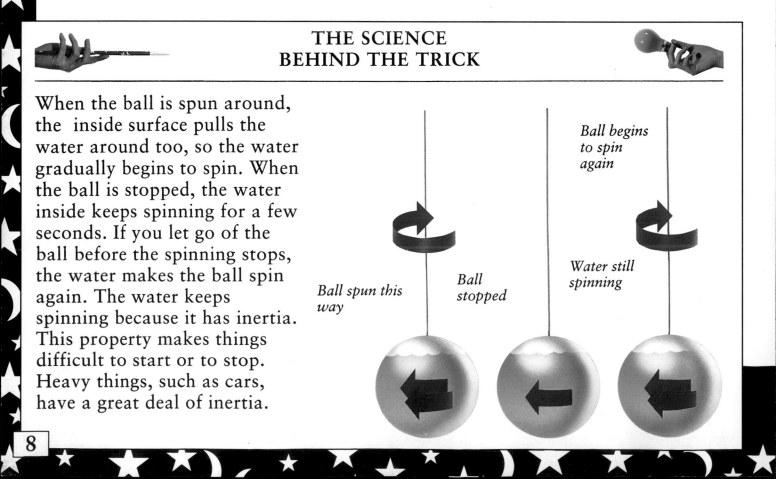

Ball spun this way

Ball stopped

Ball begins to spin again

Water still spinning

1 Make a base from the thick cardboard. It should be about 16 in. (40 cm) by 8 in. (20 cm). Bend the wire coat hanger into an L shape.

2 Push the wire into the cardboard and tape it to the base so that it stands firmly. Using the craft knife, cut a small hole in the Ping-Pong ball. Fill the ball with water.

3 Dry around the hole and seal it with the cellophane tape. Attach a long piece of thread near the hole. Tie the other end of the thread to the end of the wire.

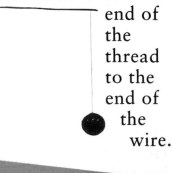

9

INTRODUCING MAGIC MARTIN
AND THE
RED ROSE GROWS TRICK

Magician or gardener? Green-thumbed Magic Martin grows a red rose during his performance.

WHAT YOU NEED
Scissors ★ Thin cardboard ★ Plastic tube Cellophane tape ★ Green paint ★ White tissue paper ★ Red food coloring ★ Cotton balls Glass vase ★ Water

This trick takes a little while to work, so begin it at the start of your show and let it work while you perform your other tricks. Pour some plain water into the vase. Wave your wand and command the rose to grow! Put the vase to one side where your audience can see it. By the end of your show the rose will magically have turned red.

THE SCIENCE BEHIND THE TRICK

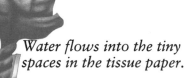

The water gradually soaks into the cotton balls and then up into the tissue paper flower. As the food coloring mixes with the water and is carried into the tissue paper, the flower turns red. The water flows into the flower because of capillary action, which draws water up into tiny spaces. There are thousands of tiny spaces between the fibers of the cotton balls and tissue paper. In real plants, water also moves up the stem to the leaves because of capillary action.

Water flows into the tiny spaces in the tissue paper.

1 Make leaves from the cardboard and attach them to the tube with the tape. Paint the tube and leaves.

2 Scrunch up a piece of tissue into a rose shape and twist the corners together. Push the twist into the top of the tube.

3 Put two drops of red food coloring into the other end of the tube, and fill the rest of the tube with the cotton balls.

4 Put the prepared flower into the glass vase. Fill a pitcher with water ready to pour into the vase.

WHAT YOU NEED
Craft knife ★ Large
plastic bottle ★ Paint
Colored paper
Scissors ★ Plastic tube
Sticky putty ★ Yellow
and red food coloring
Water ★ Plastic
container ★ Glass

INTRODUCING MAGIC MARIA
AND THE
BEWILDERING BOTTLE

The audience gasps as Magic Maria turns red into yellow with this strange bottle.

Put the Bewildering Bottle onto your table. Place the glass under the tube to catch the water. Announce that you will now change red into yellow. Carefully pour red water into the floating container. Yellow water will begin to pour out of the tube. Your audience will think that the bottle is magically changing the color of the water.

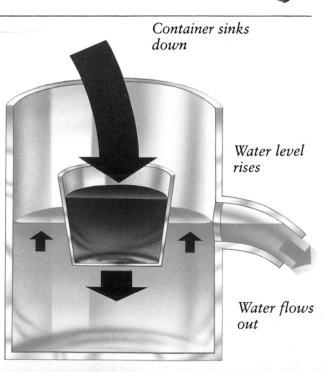

THE SCIENCE
BEHIND THE TRICK

As water is poured into the inner container, it gets heavier and it sinks further down into the yellow water, pushing it out of the way. The level of the yellow water rises until it flows out of the tube. The amount of yellow water that is pushed out of the way is the same as the amount of red water that is poured into the floating container. This is called displacement.

Container sinks down

Water level rises

Water flows out

1 Using the craft knife, carefully cut off the top of the bottle and paint it. When it is dry, cover it in a sheet of the colored paper with star shapes cut out of the paper.

2 Cut a hole in the side of the bottle, and push in a piece of plastic tube. Seal around the hole with sticky putty. Paint the tube. Fill the bottle with yellow water, and put the plastic container inside.

INTRODUCING MAGIC MALCOLM
AND THE
FAITHFUL FOUNTAIN

Magic Malcolm defies gravity to make water flow uphill and produce a fountain.

Before you start, put a glass underneath to catch the water. To start the fountain, secretly squeeze the binder clip to let the water flow. Say some magic words at the same time and tap the fountain with your magic wand. To stop the fountain, secretly let the clip close again.

WHAT YOU NEED
Drill ★ Plastic bottle
Straws ★ Sticky putty
Glue ★ Two cardboard
boxes ★ Scissors ★ Water
Binder clip ★ Glass

THE SCIENCE
BEHIND THE TRICK

When the binder clip is released, water pours down the straw from the bottle. The air in the bottle spreads out to fill the space. As a result the pressure in the bottle goes down. The greater pressure in the air outside the bottle pushes down on the water in the glass and makes the water go up the straw. The bottle works like a vacuum cleaner, "sucking" water up to make the fountain inside the bottle. When you close the clip, the water stops flowing out of the bottle. The fountain stops because the pressure is no longer going down.

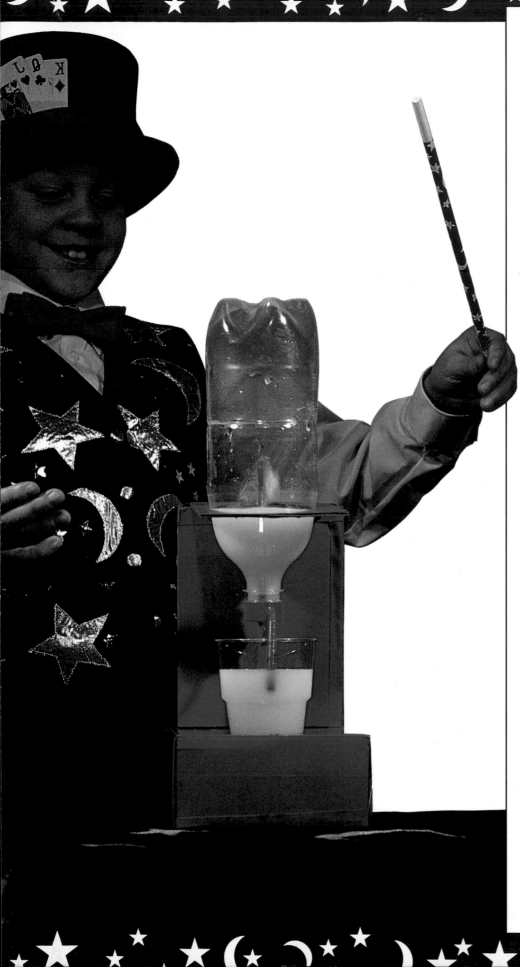

1 Drill two holes in the bottle cap. Put straws through the holes and bend them as shown. Seal around the holes with sticky putty.

2 Glue together the two cardboard boxes to make a stand. Make two small holes in the horizontal box, and feed through the longer straw.

3 Put some water in the bottle. Clip the binder clip on the longer straw. Attach the bottle and turn the stand upside down.

INTRODUCING MAGIC MANDY
AND THE
INVISIBLE DRAWING

The pictures are invisible, but Magic Mandy can see each as clear as day.

Ask the audience to call out their favorite animals. Draw the first animal with the magic pen. Then keep drawing the first animal, no matter what else is called out. For example, if the first animal called out was a dog, draw a dog every time. Put the finished drawings into the box and ask a volunteer to choose one. Say that you think the chosen picture is a dog. Using the brush and watercolors, paint over the picture. The dog will appear!

WHAT YOU NEED
Candle ★ Craft knife
Thin cardboard ★ Glue
Scissors ★ Colored paper
Cardboard box
Watercolors ★ Jar
White paper
Paintbrush

THE SCIENCE
BEHIND THE TRICK

Candle wax is made from oil. Oily things do not mix well with water. That's why wax is used to protect surfaces from water. The wax lines on the picture are invisible until the watercolor paint is added. Where there is no wax, the paint soaks into the paper, coloring it. The water runs off the wax, leaving white lines.

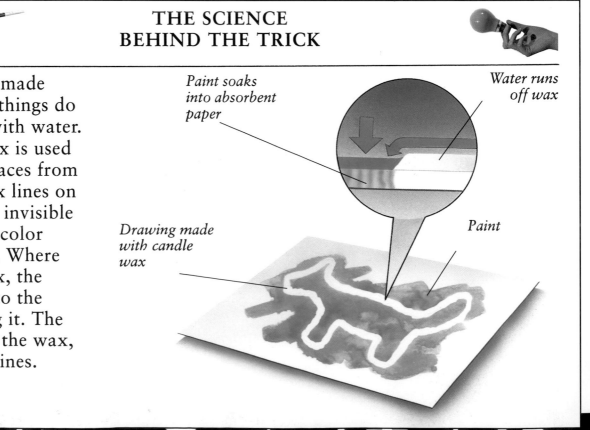

Paint soaks into absorbent paper

Water runs off wax

Drawing made with candle wax

Paint

1 Using the craft knife, sharpen the candle and cover it with the cardboard. Glue on moons and stars cut from the colored paper. This will be your magic pen.

2 Decorate the box with magic symbols. Put some of the watercolor in a jar. Have some sheets of white paper ready to draw on.

INTRODUCING MAGIC MALCOLM
AND THE
BOTTLE THAT NEVER EMPTIES

Empty or full? Magic Malcolm baffles the audience with this strange, magical bottle, also known as a Soda Bowl.

This trick makes a good "running gag" for your performance. Keep a finger over the hole, and tip the bottle over. Water will pour out into the glass. Now turn the bottle upright and tip it over again. This proves that it's "empty." Put the bottle and glass to one side and perform another trick. Later, repeat the same sequence. Amazingly, there will be more water in the bottle!

WHAT YOU NEED
Scissors ★ Plastic tube, about ⅝ in. (1.5 cm) wide ★ Plastic soda bottle ★ Thin cardboard Sticky putty ★ Food coloring ★ Water Funnel ★ Glass

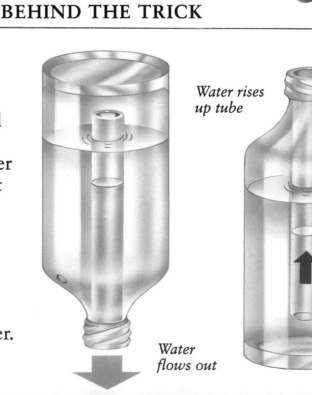

THE SCIENCE BEHIND THE TRICK

When you take your finger off the hole, water flows up the tube. The water level in the bottle goes down a bit. The water in the tube pours out when you tip the bottle over. With the hole blocked, water cannot flow up the tube because air cannot get into the space above the water.

Hole unblocked

Water rises up tube

Water flows out

1 Cut a piece of plastic tube about 1/2 in. (1 cm) less than the height of the bottle.

2 Push the tube into the bottle. Use a piece of folded cardboard to wedge the tube in. Make sure that no water can escape. Seal the tube into place with sticky putty. Paint and decorate the bottle.

3 Cut a tiny hole near the neck of the bottle. Fill the bottle with colored water, using a funnel.

19

GLASS THAT NEVER FILLS

Magic Mike has the unfillable glass under his spell. As soon as it's full, it's empty again!

Pour water into the plastic glass until it's half full. The glass will not empty yet. Now slowly fill it to the brim. Quickly tap the glass with your wand, and command it to empty. The water will magically drain away!

WHAT YOU NEED
Two cardboard boxes
Scissors ★ Paint ★ Colored
paper ★ Small bowl
Plastic glass ★ Bendable
straws ★ Sticky putty

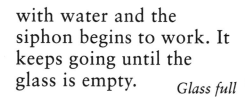

THE SCIENCE BEHIND THE TRICK

The water drains away because the straws make a siphon. When the water in the glass is deep enough, the tube fills with water and the siphon begins to work. It keeps going until the glass is empty.

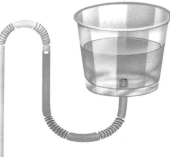

Glass half full

Siphon tube not full

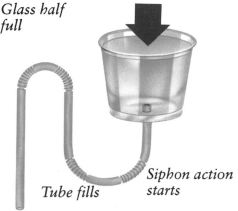

Glass full

Tube fills

Siphon action starts

1 Using two cardboard boxes, make a stand. Paint it and decorate it with cut-out stars. Place a small bowl in the bottom box.

2 Cut a small hole in the bottom of the plastic glass. Make a tube from the straws, and seal one end into the glass with the putty.

3 Make three small holes in the lower box and feed the straws through as shown.

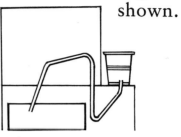

WHAT YOU NEED
Scissors ★ Thick cardboard ★ Colored paper or paints ★ Plastic tube ★ Red and yellow food coloring ★ Water

INTRODUCING MAGIC MIKE
— AND THE —
AROUND THE BEND TRICK

Magic Mike sends the audience around the bend! Is the water red or yellow?

Hold the board upright in front of you, gripping it as shown in the picture on page 23. Now announce that you can change red water into yellow simply by tilting the tubes. Tilt one way and then the other. The level will stay the same in both tubes and it will look as though the red water changes to yellow as it passes under your hands.

THE SCIENCE BEHIND THE TRICK

When the tubes are held upright, the water level is the same on each side because water always finds its own level. When you tilt the tubes, the water moves around so that the levels remain the same on both sides. The depth is the same when measured from the lowest part of the tube, even though there is now more water on one side of the tube than the other.

Lowest part of tube

Water at same depth

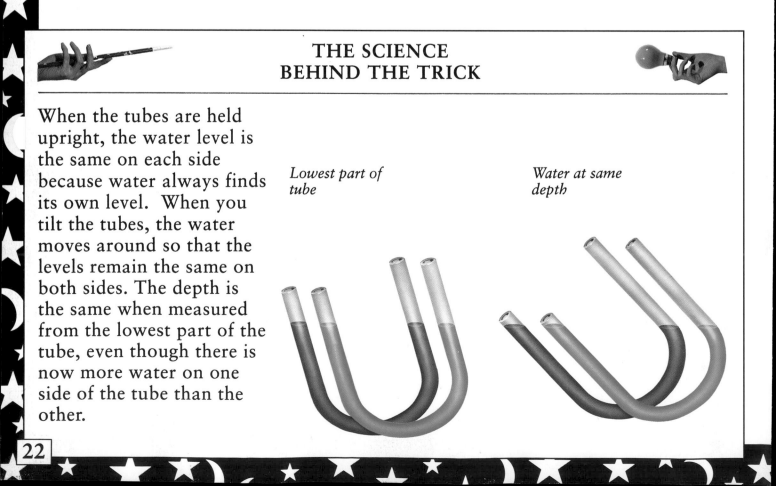

Cut a piece of cardboard about 20 in. (50 cm) by 12 in. (30 cm) and decorate. Cut two pieces of tube about 40 in. (100 cm) long. Make two holes in the cardboard and feed the tubes through. Fill the tubes to the same level with colored water, one red and one yellow. Cover the holes with cardboard.

INTRODUCING MAGIC MIKE
AND THE
SHOOTING STARS

With a flourish of his magic wand, Magic Mike sends the stars shooting through the water.

Wave your magic wand before the audience, and tell them a story about its magical powers. "Legend says that this magic wand belonged to the wizard Merlin" might be a good start. Ask a volunteer to watch the stars in the bowl. While the person is watching, secretly dip the end of the wand into the dishwashing detergent. Tap the water with the wand. The stars will shoot to the edge of the bowl.

WHAT YOU NEED
Wooden dowel about 12 in. (30 cm) long ★ Red and white paint ★ Scissors Cellophane candy wrappers Glass bowl of water ★ Glass Dishwashing detergent

THE SCIENCE BEHIND THE TRICK

Water is made up of millions of tiny particles called molecules, which cling to each other. As a result the surface of water is like a stretchy skin. The skin can support light, flat objects such as the paper stars. Detergents, such as those used to wash dishes, break down surface tension. When the detergent touches the water, the skin breaks in the middle. Surface tension pulls the stars to the edge of the bowl as the skin breaks apart.

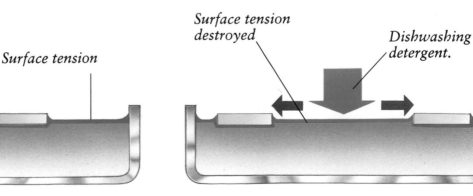

Stars — Surface tension

Surface tension destroyed — Dishwashing detergent.

Make sure no dish-washing liquid falls off the end of the wand before it touches the water.

Tap the wand right in the center of the bowl, sending the stars shooting.

GETTING PREPARED

1 Make your magic wand from the dowel. Paint the middle red and about 1¹/2 in. (4 cm) at each end white. Decorate the wand with magic symbols.

2 Cut some stars from the cellophane candy wrappers. Carefully float them in a bowl of water. Put some dish-washing detergent in a glass.

INTRODUCING MAGIC MARIA
— AND THE —
SINK OR SWIM TRICK

Magic Maria stuns the audience with an egg-raising trick!

WHAT YOU NEED
*Scissors ★ Cardboard box
Colored paper ★ Two
plastic glasses ★ Water
Salt ★ Two eggs ★ Thick
cardboard ★ Turntable
(lazy Susan)*

Start with the turntable turned so that the glass containing the unsalted water is at the front. Announce that you will now make the egg float. Cover the box with the cloth. Wave your wand over the cloth while you secretly turn the turntable. Remove the cloth to reveal a magically floating egg!

THE SCIENCE
BEHIND THE TRICK

Whether an object floats or sinks depends on its density, that is, its mass per unit volume. An egg is slightly denser than plain water. This means that it sinks to the bottom of a glass. Adding salt to water makes the water more dense. When enough salt is added, the water becomes more dense than the egg. Then the egg floats instead of sinking.

Salt water

Plain water

*Egg more
dense than
water*

*Egg less
dense than
water*

1 Cut the top and bottom off the box, and decorate it with stars cut from the paper.

2 Fill one plastic glass with plain water and the other with salt water.

3 Make a divider. Decorate the front and back the same way. Tape it to the turntable. Put both in the box.

HINTS AND TIPS

Here are some hints and tips for making your props. Good props will make your act look more professional, so spend time making and decorating your props, and look after them carefully. As well as the special props you need for each trick, try to make some general props such as a vest and a magic wand.

Decorate your props with magic shapes cut from colored paper. Paint bottles and tubes with oil-based paint.

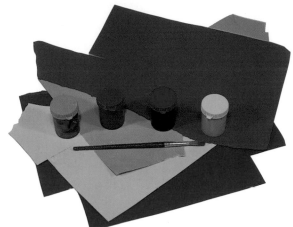

Make colored water by adding food coloring to tap water. You need only a few drops of coloring in a pitcher of water.

You will need cellophane tape and glue to make props. Double-sided tape may also be useful. You can use sticky putty or special plastic sealant to make waterproof joints.

Try cutting magic shapes out of cardboard and using the holes to make stencils.

Your act will look more professional if you make a stage setting. This is easy if you have a backdrop to hang behind the stage. A large piece of black cloth is most effective. Use silver paint to create stars and moons. Also decorate pieces of cloth to throw over your table. The overall effect will be dramatic, creating an atmosphere of mystery and magic.

Make your own magician's clothes. Try to find an old hat and vest to decorate. If you can find some silvery material, cut out stars and moons and sew them on. An alternative is to use sequins or anything else that is shiny and dramatic so you look professional.

Table

Backdrop

Cloth

Assistant's table

Make a magician's table by draping a cloth over an ordinary table. You can put the props out of sight underneath.

GLOSSARY

CAPILLARY ACTION The rising or falling of water in contact with a solid.

DENSITY The mass of a particular volume of a substance.

DISPLACEMENT The amount of water pushed aside by an object that is immersed or floating.

INERTIA The resistance of an object to any change of direction or movement.

MOLECULES The smallest naturally occurring particles of a substance.

PRESSURE The squeezing that results when force is applied to a substance and there is no room for the substance to change shape.

SIPHON ACTION The force that causes a liquid to flow through a narrow tube because of differences in pressure.

SURFACE TENSION The molecular force of a liquid that pulls the liquid into the smallest possible area, making water drops and forming a curved surface (meniscus) on a glass of water.

INDEX